I0410070

I AM
A Lot of Things

by Dianna L Grayer, Ph.D.

Illustrated by Sierra Atkins

Book Cover Design: Samantha Lane and Dianna L. Grayer
Book Cover Art and interior illustrations: Sierra Atkins
Book Layout: Samantha Lane and Dianna L. Grayer
Edited by: Deborah Berk

Printed in the United States of America

ISBN13: 978-1466224667
Library of Congress Control Number: 2011914955

This book is dedicated to all the youngsters who are growing and becoming. Know that you can feel good about yourself and achieve your dreams because you are a lot of things!

I want to thank 10 year old Sierra Atkins for her beautiful illustrations throughout the book. Sierra knew I was looking for someone to illustrate another one of my children's books so she took the initiative, drew an image, and shared it with me. Unfortunately I had already contracted another illustrator for that particular book but I was so impressed with Sierra's initiative that I wanted to give her an opportunity to illustrate her first children's book. I looked through my collection of manuscripts and invited Sierra to illustrate, *I Am a Lot of Things*, because she is definitely a lot of things! Also, a huge thank you to Samantha Lane who was able to take Sierra's illustrations and placed them so beautifully throughout these pages.

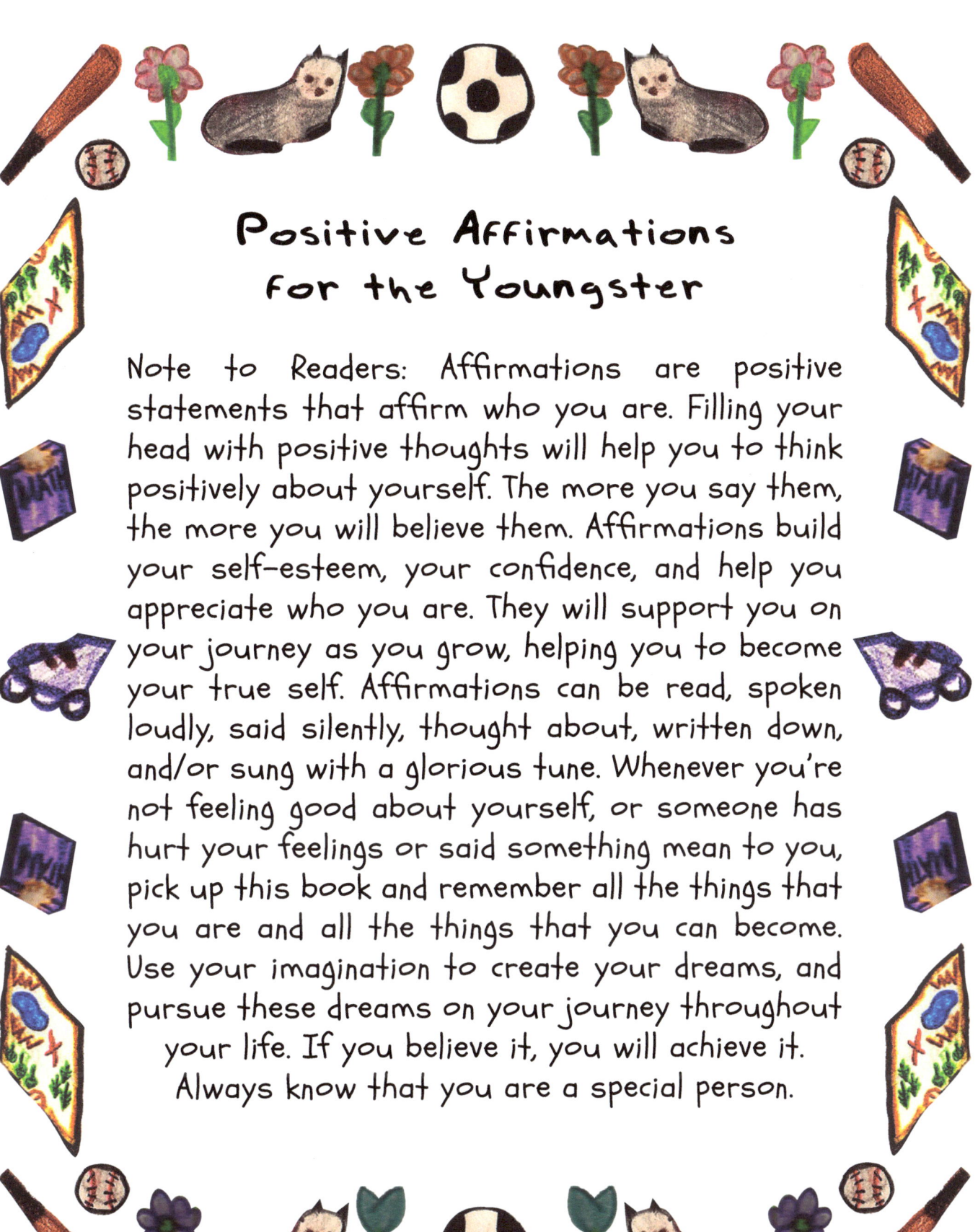

Positive Affirmations for the Youngster

Note to Readers: Affirmations are positive statements that affirm who you are. Filling your head with positive thoughts will help you to think positively about yourself. The more you say them, the more you will believe them. Affirmations build your self-esteem, your confidence, and help you appreciate who you are. They will support you on your journey as you grow, helping you to become your true self. Affirmations can be read, spoken loudly, said silently, thought about, written down, and/or sung with a glorious tune. Whenever you're not feeling good about yourself, or someone has hurt your feelings or said something mean to you, pick up this book and remember all the things that you are and all the things that you can become. Use your imagination to create your dreams, and pursue these dreams on your journey throughout your life. If you believe it, you will achieve it. Always know that you are a special person.

I AM SMART!

I AM SMART because I can use my brain to learn anything I want to learn. I can learn my schoolwork like math, spelling, and reading. I am so smart, I can earn good grades in school and become a doctor, a lawyer, a CEO of a company, a teacher, or a therapist. I can even become the President of the United States. I can learn how to play games, how to cook, how to make things grow, how to build things, how to take care of myself, or how to be the lead in a play. And, when I don't understand something,

I can ask for help so that I do understand, or I can research it on the computer. Whatever I want to do in my life, I can learn to do it because I AM SMART!

I AM STRONG!

    I AM STRONG in two different ways: One way is with my muscles—I can pick up my toys, carry my things, and help to clean up around the house. I can lift and hold my dog and cat in my arms. The other way that I am strong is with my mind—I am going to do my best, even when people say that I can't do something or when they tease me. I am strong. Their words might hurt me somewhat, but they will not damage me. Because I am strong, I can use my voice and tell them to stop being mean. I have a strong mind which can help to motivate me to excel in

sports or to achieve my goals; things that I want to do like ride my bike a specific distance. Being strong gives me the ability to take care of myself. When I take care of myself and when I help out at home, I AM STRONG!

I AM COURAGEOUS!

10 x 1 =   10 x 4 =
10 x 2 =   10 x 5 =
10 x 3 =   10 x 6 =

I AM COURAGEOUS because I can sleep in the dark. I am courageous whenever I try something new, like tasting different foods, holding a pet snake, roller-blading, snow boarding or jumping off of the diving board. I am courageous when my teacher asks me to come to the front of the room to do a math problem or to read a

story aloud. Talking and sharing with others can be scary, but I know it's important for me to share my thoughts and feelings with others. It tells them that I'm important and that I matter. So when I let others see who I am by sharing something about myself, then I AM COURAGEOUS!

Food Samples

I AM FUNNY!

I AM FUNNY because I love to play and laugh. I do funny things to entertain my family. We take turns making funny faces and telling silly jokes. Sometimes, I say things that I don't mean to be funny, but they are. When everybody else laughs, I laugh at myself, too. I laugh, and then, I laugh some more. I never, ever want to stop laughing. When I laugh, I feel good all over. I like it when something funny happens because it stores in my memory forever. And, I can think about it whenever I

want to have a good laugh all over again. I also like to play and laugh with my friends, because they are so funny. But, best of all, I like myself because I AM FUNNY!

I AM HONEST!

 I AM HONEST because I tell the truth. Lying is wrong, and it feels bad, too. I want to be trustworthy, and I want others to believe what I say. When I make a habit of telling the truth, everyone will believe what I say, including my family, my friends, and my teachers. They will all trust me. I do not disturb anything without asking permission first. I do not take things that belong to others because I know that it is wrong to steal. If I want something, I ask my parents to buy it for me, and if they can't, or won't, I will find a way to earn the money so that I can buy it for myself. I will follow the rules and do the right thing because it makes me feel good inside. People trust me because I am honest. I love that I AM HONEST!

I AM LOVEABLE!

    I AM LOVEABLE because I am cuddly, kind, and fun. I am loving and caring as well, and I have a fantastic sense of humor. My parents love me, and they make me feel special inside and out. When they spend time with me and play with me, it makes me feel loveable and makes me able to love myself. I love myself very much, which makes me feel that I am loveable to others. Sometimes, when my parents can't play with me, it makes me sad. However, it doesn't mean that I'm not loveable. I am loveable because I have a great personality. People like being around me because I make them feel loveable. And, when others are

loveable and nice toward me, it makes me feel loveable in return. We keep passing these good, loveable feelings back and forth. It feels good to feel cared about. Sometimes, I might feel that people don't care about me, but I must remember that I am a good person and that people do care about me, and I AM LOVEABLE!

I AM RESPONSIBLE!

    I AM RESPONSIBLE because I know how to take care of my duties. I can keep my room clean, and I can do all of my chores. I know that when I take my toys out and play with them, I can put them neatly back, where they belong. I can do my homework or any job that I am given well. I can go to sleep when it's my bedtime and wake up on time to get myself ready for school. I can pick out my clothes and have them ready when I wake up. I can brush my teeth, wash my face, eat my breakfast, and clean my room all before I head off to school. My parents are

proud of me when I take care of all of my chores and duties, especially when I do them well and with pride. When I do my best, I feel good about myself, and I know that I AM RESPONSIBLE!

I AM RESPECTFUL!

I AM RESPECTFUL because I respect people and their things, and I respect all of the animals and the earth. I am respectful of all adults, especially my parents and my teachers. I respect all companion animals or pets and the other animals that I see around me, even snakes and spiders. They deserve to live, too. I respect the earth, and so, I do not litter and make it ugly and dirty. I will put my trash in the garbage at all times. Even when I'm out playing and there is no garbage can around me, I will save my candy wrappers, soda cans, or ice cream sticks until I'm able to find a trash can to put them in. I will put all of my recyclables in the right containers. I also

show that I respect myself by the actions that I take; I understand that there will be consequences for my actions, so I don't hurt myself or purposefully get into trouble. I know that if this happened, my teacher or my parents may get mad at me, and that would make me feel bad. I know that making mistakes is part of growing up, but I am aware that there are lessons to be learned from these mistakes, and because I respect myself, I will attempt to learn my lessons quickly and not repeat my mistakes. When I'm respectful toward others, I gain respect from them as well. I feel good about myself when I AM RESPECTFUL!

I AM UNIQUE!

I AM UNIQUE because there is no one like me and this is fantastic! I like who I am. I might not talk or look like others, and that's okay with me. I might even wear my hair different and dress in my very own style, and that's okay, too. My differences and everyone else's differences are what help to make the world a more interesting place. I am one petal of a flower of the many flowers that cover the earth over the many areas of the world. It would be strange if we all looked alike or if all petals were the same. We wouldn't know one person from another

because they would all seem to look the same. I like being unique—my own self. I can do things in my own way, which may be different from the way that other people do them, but I can still do a good job. It's okay to be different. I accept all of my differences, which are all unique to me. The way that I talk, laugh, and write are all parts of my uniqueness. My skin color, eyes, and hair are all unique parts of me. All that matters is that I'm perfect just the way I am. I am happy that I AM UNIQUE!

23

I AM TALENTED!

    I AM TALENTED because I have hobbies and varied interests. I can sing, dance, play sports, play an instrument, paint pictures, write poems and stories, and stand on my head. I can learn new things whenever I want to give them a try. I will be great at some things, and I will be okay at others. The ones that I am great at will make me proud of my ability and creativity. My talents are my very own; they represent who I am, what I enjoy and what I am about. I love to share my talents with others because I want them to know who I am. When people know who

I am, they will find out how interesting I am. If I'm shy, people won't get to know me, and then, I don't get to know them. I will share myself because I'm proud of the person I am and of all the special things that I can do. I am very happy that I AM TALENTED!

I AM A LEADER!

    I AM A LEADER because I have good ideas and because I want to share them with others. When I talk, people listen, and when others talk, I listen. When I take care of myself, be respectful, and do the right thing, I am in the position of becoming a role model for other people. I can teach them new things and offer help when they need it. Sometimes, people may say things that are not nice or respectful. These words might be hurtful, and I know that it is okay to let them know how they made me or someone else feel in these situations. I can also share other ways, perhaps better ways, to express their feelings

rather than to say hurtful things. I am not afraid—I am courageous. I am also honest and trustworthy. These skills represent that I AM A LEADER!

I AM SPECIAL!

I AM SPECIAL for being who I am. Just being me makes me special. I like myself and who I am, and that makes me special. My family loves me, and that makes me feel special, too. When they spend time with me, I feel really special. Even if they don't spend as much time as I want them to, I am still special. I feel special when I receive an award or hit a homerun or receive a compliment.

I feel special when my family teaches me important and fun things like how to cook, play games, play sports. I feel special when I'm acknowledged for doing a good job and for being thoughtful and kind. I am a good person. I love myself and I am loved by others, so I AM SPECIAL!

This book tells me that I AM A LOT OF THINGS! I am me. I can do anything and be anything that I want to be. I have many wonderful traits and I will remind myself of them by repeating them—or affirming them—every day. They will help me grow to be a Smart, Strong, Courageous, Funny, Honest, Loveable, Responsible, Respectful, Unique, and Talented Leader, who is somebody Special! And, as I grow up, there will be many more parts of me that I will discover and become—because I AM A LOT OF THINGS!

31

I AM A LOT OF THINGS DISCOVERY WORKSHEET

Fill in the blanks below to learn things you might not have known about yourself. Share all the ways that you are a lot of things. For the younger kids please tell them all the ways you see them.

I am SMART! Share ways that I am SMART.

1. _____
2. _____
3. _____
4. _____
5. _____

I am STRONG! Share ways that I am STRONG.

1. _____
2. _____
3. _____
4. _____
5. _____

I am COURAGEOUS! Share ways that I am COURAGEOUS.

1. _____
2. _____
3. _____
4. _____
5. _____

I am FUNNY! Share ways that I am FUNNY.

1. _____
2. _____
3. _____
4. _____
5. _____

I am HONEST! Share ways that I am HONEST.

1. _____
2. _____
3. _____
4. _____
5. _____

I am LOVEABLE! Share ways that I am LOVEABLE.

1. _____
2. _____
3. _____
4. _____
5. _____

I am RESPONSIBLE! Share ways that I am RESPONSIBLE.

1. _____
2. _____
3. _____
4. _____
5. _____

I am RESPECTFUL! Share ways that I am RESPECTFUL

1. _____
2. _____
3. _____
4. _____
5. _____

I am UNIQUE! Share ways that I am UNIQUE.

1. _____
2. _____
3. _____
4. _____
5. _____

I am TALENTED! Share ways that I am TALENTED.

1. _____
2. _____
3. _____
4. _____
5. _____

I am a LEADER! Share ways that I am a LEADER.

1. _____
2. _____
3. _____
4. _____
5. _____

I am SPECIAL! Share ways that I am SPECIAL

1. _____
2. _____
3. _____
4. _____
5. _____

Add more when you discover them.
Good Work!!!!!!! Remember to play, laugh, and have fun!

ABOUT THE AUTHOR

DIANNA L GRAYER, Ph.D., is a Marriage and Family Therapist in Northern California. She has counseled children, teens, adults, couples, and families from diverse backgrounds for over 16 years, and continues to do so. Dianna loves supporting, encouraging, and teaching others to care more deeply for themselves, to live fuller and happier lives, and to meet their full potential. In 2010, she earned her Ph.D. in Psychology from Meridian University, where she serves as a faculty member. She lives with her partner of over 34 years, and together, they have fostered 26 children. When she's not seeing clients or teaching, Dianna spends most of her time writing children's stories and poems, creating tools and workshops to help people heal their lives, playing basketball and games, laughing, and enjoying nature.

ABOUT THE ILLUSTRATOR

SIERRA KAI ATKINS was born in Santa Rosa, California, and she is in the 5th grade. She lives with her parents and her pet fish, Swimly. Besides drawing, Sierra enjoys writing, camping, playing with her friends, climbing trees, and inventing potions. She also loves playing basketball and soccer. She is funny, creative, and has an outgoing personality. Sierra hopes to illustrate more books in the future!

Also by Dianna L. Grayer, Ph.D.

The Lone Bird

Deonna's Unveiling
A Girl, A Teacher, A Turtle and An Eagle

www.drdiannagrayer.com

www.ingramcontent.com/pod-product-compliance
Lightning Source LLC
Chambersburg PA
CBHW040307010626
45792CB00025B/1432